Piece of cake

First English edition for North America published by
Barron's Educational Series, Inc., 2004.

First published by **MQ Publications Limited**
12 The Ivories, 6-8 Northampton Street, London, England

Editor: **Tracy Hopkins**
Design: **Lindsey Johns**

All inquiries should be addressed to:
Barron's Educational Series, Inc.
250 Wireless Boulevard
Hauppage, New York 11788
http://www.barronseduc.com

International Standard Book No. 0-7641-5722-1
Library of Congress Catalog Card No. 2003107441

Printed and bound in China
9 8 7 6 5 4 3 2 1

Contents

Introduction

A slice of homemade cake is one of life's simplest pleasures, so why do so many of us buy cakes instead of baking them? It's time to forget the supermarket and to return the cake mixes to their boxes. Let's remind ourselves just how easy and enjoyable it is to bake our own mouthwatering spongecakes, muffins, tortes, and cupcakes.

By following the simple step-by-step instructions, you can bake traditional homemade cakes just like Grandma used to make. Get back to basics with true American classics—from much-loved chocolate chip muffins and classic baked cheesecake to a light and airy angel food cake. Give your family a taste of home cooking with a cake tailor-made for any celebration: a chocolate roulade that's perfect for Christmas, a baked Alaska for topping with birthday candles, and an elegant chocolate and raspberry torte to dazzle your dinner guests.

With a little practice, you'll soon be mastering the art of baking and adding your own modern twists to these timeless recipes. Let's keep the tradition of cake-making alive and pass these skills on to our children. Maybe one day they'll be creating delicious Bake-Off winning recipes of their own.

The Basics

When following any cake recipe it is important to remember a few basic rules. First, preheat the oven before you start to allow it to reach the required temperature. Next, read through the recipe to ensure you have all the ingredients. Measure out the ingredients into separate containers so they are ready to be added with the minimum of fuss. Use a set of measuring spoons and level off the surface with the back of a knife. The most important rule to remember is to ensure that all your ingredients are at room temperature before starting. Remove eggs and butter from the fridge at least two hours before cooking, or even the night before.

Creaming Method

The simplest cake making technique is the creaming method. It produces cakes with a light, fluffy, moist texture, like the lemon and poppy seed cake and the plum and amaretti sponge slices. You'll find the majority of cake recipes begin with creaming butter and sugar together. This can be done with a wooden spoon or more simply with a hand-held electric mixer. The mixture should become pale, light, and fluffy in appearance, it shouldn't be the least bit grainy, and it should resemble smooth whipped cream. At this stage the beaten eggs should be added gradually and beaten well after each addition to prevent the mixture from curdling. A spoonful of the measured out flour can be added with the last addition of egg as a precaution against curdling. The remaining flour and any other ingredients should be gently folded in by hand with a metal spoon.

All-in-One Method

This method means just that. All the main ingredients go into a bowl and are beaten together using a hand-held electric mixer or tabletop mixer until soft and creamy. If the butter is very soft, the ingredients can be beaten by hand, but this can be very hard work. It is important that the butter is very soft to ensure even blending and that extra leavening, such as baking powder, is used to compensate for the lack of air usually incorporated at the creaming stage. This method produces cakes with a slightly closer texture. It is used for the frosted lime bars and the peanut butter slices.

Beating Method

This method produces cakes with the lightest texture but the shortest keeping time, such as the angel food cake and walnut and strawberry celebration cake. The initial beating stage is crucial to the success of the finished cake. Use eggs and sugar at room temperature for the best volume. They should be beaten together, preferably with a tabletop mixer or hand-held electric mixer, until the mixture is thick and foamy and has reached the ribbon stage. The best way to test for this stage is to turn off the mixer and lift it out of the batter. As the mixture runs off the beaters, use it to write your initial over the top of the mixture in the bowl. If you can still read it when you have finished writing, the ribbon stage has been reached. You can now add the flour, using a swift but light folding action with a large spoon. Resist the urge to bang the beaters on the edge of the bowl; this will knock air out of the mixture. You can speed up this method by placing the mixing bowl over a saucepan of hot water while beating. When the ribbon stage has been reached, take the bowl off the heat and continue beating until the mixture is cool.

Lining Pans

Line your cake pan before preparing the mixture so the cake can go straight into the oven with no delay. Melted vegetable shortening is the best thing to use when greasing pans. Use a pastry brush to brush a thin layer over the inside of the pan.
Bases: Most cake recipes only require the bottom of the pan to be lined with waxed paper. Place the pan on a double folded sheet of paper and draw around the pan with a pencil. Cut out the shape inside the pencil mark to give two circles or squares and place both pieces in the base of the pan. Alternatively, precut bases can be bought for ease.
Sides: Cut a double strip of waxed paper long enough to reach around the pan and high enough to

extend 1 inch (2.5 cm) above the top. Fold one edge of the strip over by 1 inch (2.5 cm), then use scissors to snip cuts at 1-inch (2.5-cm) intervals along its length. Place the snipped edge into the bottom of the pan using a greased pastry brush to push the fold into the bottom corners. Top the snipped sections with the cut bases.

Testing Cakes

The center of the cake is the last part to be cooked, so test the center once the cooking time is up.

- With sponge cakes a gentle touch of the top will tell you if the cake is cooked. If your fingertips leave no impression and the mixture springs back, the cake is done. The mixture will also have started to pull away from the sides of the pan.
- For heavier cakes with ground almonds or dried fruit, a skewer test is best. Insert a thin skewer into the center of the cake. When removed, it should have no batter stuck to it.
- Another quick and easy way is to listen to the cake. If you can hear bubbling noises, the cake is not cooked.

Storing Cakes

The best way to store cakes is to freeze them on the day of baking.

- Leave heavier cakes in their lining paper and then overwrap with plastic wrap or seal in a freezer bag. Wrap sponge cakes in waxed paper, then overwrap in plastic wrap or seal in a freezer bag.
- For short-term storage, place cooled cakes in an airtight container.
- Keep cakes with fresh cream fillings in the refrigerator.
- Fatless spongecakes will keep for 1–2 days; other beaten sponges, 3 days; creamed mixtures, 1 week; light fruit cakes, 2 weeks; rich fruit cakes, if stored well, 2–3 months.

Family Cakes

Pound Cake

This classic cake has a fine texture
and is delicately flavored with fresh
lemon peel. It's bound to be a huge
hit with all the family.

Serves 10–12

1 rounded cup (250 g) butter, softened
1¼ cups (275 g) sugar
grated peel of 1 lemon
5 eggs, lightly beaten
2¼ cups (250 g) all-purpose flour
1 tsp. baking powder
½ tsp. salt
½ cup (125 ml) milk
confectioners' sugar, for dusting

1 Preheat the oven to 300°F (150°C,
Gas 2). Lightly grease a nonstick 12-cup
Bundt pan or a kugelhopf mold.

2 Cream the butter and sugar together
until light and fluffy. Beat in the lemon
peel. Add the eggs, a little at a time,
beating well after each addition. Sift the
flour and baking powder together and
gradually add.

3 Add the salt and milk and mix
thoroughly. The mixture may appear
curdled—this is okay. Pour into the
prepared pan and level the surface.

4 Bake in the center of the oven until
the cake is risen and golden and a
toothpick inserted in the middle comes
out clean, about 1 hour, 20 minutes.
Check after 1 hour, and if the top is very
brown, cover loosely with aluminum foil.

5 Let cool in the pan 10 minutes, then
turn out onto a wire rack and let cool
completely. Dust the cake lightly with
confectioners' sugar before slicing.

Lemon and Poppy Seed Cake

This poppy seed cake is moistened with a tangy lemon syrup after it's baked to give it a really delicious texture. It keeps well in an airtight container for up to a week.

Serves 6–8

3/4 cup (175 g) butter
3/4 cup (175 g) sugar
3 eggs, beaten
1 1/2 cups (175 g) all-purpose flour
2 tsp. baking powder
1 tbsp. poppy seeds
2 tsp. grated lemon peel

Syrup
3 tbsp. sugar
juice of 1 lemon

1 Preheat the oven to 350°F (180°C, Gas 4). Grease and bottom-line an 8 1/2 x 4 1/2 x 3 1/2-in. (21 x 10 x 7.5-cm) loaf pan.

2 Cream the butter and sugar together until light and fluffy. Gradually beat in the eggs, a little at a time. Sift the flour and baking powder together, then fold in with the poppy seeds and lemon peel.

3 Pour the mixture into the prepared pan and bake until the cake is risen and golden and a skewer inserted in the center comes out clean, 1 1/4 to 1 1/2 hours. Remove the cake from the oven but leave in the pan.

4 To make the syrup, gently heat the sugar and lemon juice together until the sugar has dissolved. Bring to a boil, then pour the mixture over the cake and let cool. Cut into slices to serve.

Iced Lemon and Ginger Cake

A homemade cake is an essential part of a family picnic, and this deliciously sticky, dark treat will have them all clamoring for more. It improves with age, so it's best to make it in advance.

Serves 6–8

2¼ cups (250 g) all-purpose flour
2 tsp. ground ginger
1 tsp. cinnamon
2 tsp. baking powder
pinch of salt
½ cup (120 g) unsalted butter
⅔ cup (135 g) packed brown sugar
1 cup (250 ml) light corn syrup
1 cup (250 ml) molasses
3 pieces crystallized ginger,
   finely chopped
½ cup (125 ml) milk
2 eggs, beaten

Frosting
2–3 tbsp. fresh lemon juice
1 cup (120 g) confectioners' sugar, sifted

1 Preheat the oven to 325°F (170°C, Gas 3). Grease and bottom-line a deep 8 x 10-in. (20 x 25-cm) cake pan.

2 Mix the flour, ginger, cinnamon, baking powder, and salt in a large bowl.

3 Place the butter, sugar, syrup, and molasses in a saucepan and heat gently until melted. Beat the mixture into the dry ingredients. Stir in the crystallized ginger and milk, then beat in the eggs.

4 Pour the mixture into the prepared pan and bake 1 hour. Let cool before turning out.

5 To make the frosting, beat together the lemon juice and confectioners' sugar—it needs to be fairly thick so you may need to add extra sugar to reach the required consistency. Pour the frosting over the cake and let cool.

Coffee, Maple, and Pecan Sponge Cake

In this cake, whole eggs are whisked with sugar over hot water until the ribbon stage. Melted butter is also added to the cake mixture to increase richness and to improve its keeping properties.

Serves 6–8

1/2 cup (75 g) all-purpose flour
pinch of salt
3 tbsp. unsalted butter
3 large eggs
1/3 cup (75 g) sugar
1 tsp. instant coffee powder
1 tbsp. hot water
1/2 tsp. vanilla extract

Frosting
3/4 cup (175 g) butter
scant 1 cup (100 g) confectioners' sugar
1 tsp. instant coffee powder
1 tbsp. hot water
1/4 (60 ml) cup maple syrup
pecan halves, to decorate

1 Preheat the oven to 350°F (180°C, Gas 4). Grease and bottom-line an 8-in. (20-cm) cake pan.

2 Sift the flour and salt together three times and set aside. Melt the butter.

3 Break the eggs into a large heatproof bowl and add the sugar. Place the bowl over a pan of simmering water and beat until the mixture leaves a trail when lifted out of the bowl (ribbon stage). Remove from the heat.

4 Dissolve the coffee powder in the hot water. Whisk the coffee and the vanilla extract into the egg, then add the sifted flour in three batches, drizzling a little butter around the bowl between batches, and folding in. Leave any white sediment at the bottom of the saucepan.

5 Pour the mixture into the prepared cake pan and bake until golden and the top springs back when pressed lightly, 25 to 30 minutes. Let cool 2 to 3 minutes in the pan, then turn out onto a wire rack to cool completely.

6 To make the frosting, beat the butter and sugar together until pale and fluffy. Dissolve the coffee powder in the hot water, then gradually beat into the frosting with the maple syrup until light and smooth.

7 Slice the cake twice horizontally to make three layers and spread frosting over each layer. Assemble the cake and then spread the remaining frosting around the sides and on top. Decorate with pecans.

Colombia and Brazil are the world's largest producers of coffee today, but coffee beans are thought to have originated in Ethiopia. The beans were first made into a drink—*gahwa*, which means "that which prevents sleep"—in Arabia in around the 6th century. However, it was not until the 16th century that Arabian traders and pilgrims introduced their stimulating drink to Europe.

Orange and Almond Sponge Cake

This delicious moist sponge cake, filled with cream cheese flavored with fresh, tangy oranges, is great as an afternoon treat for adults and children alike.

Serves 6–8

¾ cup (175 g) butter
¾ cup (175 g) sugar
3 eggs
1¼ cups (145 g) all-purpose flour, sifted
1 tsp. baking powder
⅓ cup (40 g) ground almonds
a few drops almond extract

Frosting
11 oz. (300 g) cream cheese
2 tbsp. fresh orange juice
2 tsp. grated orange peel
scant 1 cup (100 g) confectioners'
  sugar, sifted
toasted slivered almonds and shredded
  orange peel, to decorate

1 Preheat the oven to 375°F (190°C, Gas 5). Grease and bottom-line two 8-in. (20-cm) cake pans.

2 Beat the butter and sugar together with a hand-held electric mixer until pale and fluffy.

3 Beat the eggs, then gradually beat into the butter and sugar mixture. Fold in the sifted flour, baking powder, almonds, and almond extract until combined.

4 Spoon the mixture into the pans and level the surface. Bake until golden and the centers of the cakes spring back when pressed lightly, 20 to 25 minutes.

5 Turn out of the pans and let cool on a wire rack. Meanwhile, make the frosting. Beat the cream cheese in a bowl to soften. Add the orange juice, orange peel, and confectioners' sugar, and beat until smooth and creamy.

6 Sandwich the cakes together with a little of the frosting, and use a narrow spatula or palette knife to spread the rest of the frosting over the top. Scatter toasted slivered almonds and orange peel over the top to decorate.

Simple Almond Cake

A light, moist cake packed with ground almonds, this is delicious filled with fresh fruit and cream. Choose whichever fruit you prefer and serve with whipped cream for added luxury.

Serves 6–8

1²/₃ cups (215 g) ground almonds
2 tbsp. all-purpose flour, sifted
7 large egg whites
scant 1 cup (200 g) sugar
confectioners' sugar, for dusting

Filling
2 tbsp. orange liqueur
¹/₂ cup (125 ml) heavy cream, whipped
6 oz. (175 g) strawberries, sliced

1 Preheat the oven to 350°F (180°C, Gas 4). Grease and bottom-line a 9-in. (23-cm) springform pan.

2 Sift the almonds and flour together into a bowl and set aside. Beat the egg whites in a bowl until they form stiff peaks. Gradually beat in the sugar to form a stiff and glossy meringue.

3 Gently fold in the flour and almond mixture. Spoon into the prepared pan and bake until golden and spongy to the touch, 25 to 30 minutes.

4 Let cool in the pan, then turn out and slice through horizontally. Drizzle the orange liqueur over each half. Spread one half with the whipped cream and top with the sliced strawberries. Top with the second half and dust with confectioners' sugar before serving.

CALIFORNIA ALMOND FESTIVALS

The state of California is the world's largest producer of over 100 varieties of almonds, growing 80% of the world's almond supply. The remaining crops come from the Mediterranean. The large Jordan almond from Spain is often considered to be the finest cultivated variety of the nut.

Sacramento, California, is home to both the world's biggest almond factory and the California State Fair, so it's no wonder that delicious California almonds are always featured at the massive annual event. The local almonds are a popular ingredient in many of the entrants' recipes in the extremely competitive baking events and cookery competitions.

The Capay Valley region and the town of Oakley take their love of almonds even further, holding festivals dedicated purely to the nut! The annual Oakley Almond Festival celebrates the local crop with all sorts of almond-orientated events, including a parade, a fun run, and the all-important Almond Recipe Contest. This is a fantastic community event open to the whole family, and all kinds of dishes are welcome, so long as they make good use of the delicious local almonds. Almond cakes are always favorite entries, so why not create your own cake recipe and join in the fun at Oakley this fall?

"A compromise is the art of dividing a cake in such a way that everyone believes he has the biggest piece."

Ludwig Erhard

Rhubarb and Ginger Cake

Banish the blues with this warming and delicious cake. The cornmeal adds an interesting texture and color to this cake, but ground almonds could be used instead.

Serves 6–8

1¾ cups (200 g) all-purpose flour
2 tsp. baking powder
¼ tsp. salt
⅔ cup (80 g) stone-ground cornmeal
2 eggs
½ cup (120 g) butter or margarine,
    softened
½ cup (120 g) sugar
3 tbsp. milk
1 tsp. vanilla extract
1 lb. (450 g) rhubarb, trimmed and
    cut into chunks
3 tbsp. preserved ginger in syrup,
    drained and sliced

Topping
½ cup (75 g) all-purpose flour
¼ cup (30 g) ground hazelnuts
5 tbsp. light brown sugar
½ tsp. ground ginger
¼ cup (60 g) butter, diced
confectioners' sugar, for dusting
vanilla ice cream, plain yogurt,
    or crème fraîche, to serve

1 Preheat the oven to 325°F (160°C, Gas 3). Grease and bottom-line a 9-in. (23-cm) springform pan.

2 Sift the flour, baking powder, and salt into a bowl. Stir in the cornmeal. Beat the eggs until thick, pale, and fluffy.

3 In a separate bowl, cream the butter or margarine with the sugar until light and fluffy. Fold in the dry ingredients alternately with the beaten eggs, milk, and vanilla extract to make a thick batter.

4 Spoon the mixture into the prepared pan and level the surface. Arrange the rhubarb and preserved ginger on top.

5 To make the topping, mix the flour, hazelnuts, brown sugar, and ground ginger in a bowl. Rub in the butter until the mixture looks like coarse crumbs.

6 Sprinkle the crumbs over the rhubarb and preserved ginger so that some pieces of rhubarb are quite thickly coated, while others are just dusted with the mixture.

7 Bake until the cake is firm and the crumb topping golden, 1 to 1¼ hours.

8 Test that the rhubarb is tender by gently inserting a skewer into one of the exposed pieces. Let stand in the pan 5 minutes, then remove the sides and transfer the cake to a plate.

9 Dust with confectioners' sugar and serve warm with ice cream, plain yogurt, or crème fraîche.

Rhubarb is an ancient plant that was used at least 4,000 years ago by the Chinese as a medicine because of its laxative qualities! By the early 16th century, it was being grown in Britain as an ornamental plant and a medicine, but it was not introduced into America until the early 19th century. Sweetened rhubarb is now a popular ingredient in pies, cakes, and puddings.

Apricot Frangipane Cake

This cake has a wonderful consistency and flavor. Combining apricots and almonds is nothing new, but the partnership works so well that it is always worth repeating.

Serves 6

½ cup (120 g) butter or margarine, softened
½ cup (120 g) sugar
½ tsp. almond extract
¾ cup (100 g) all-purpose flour
1 tsp. baking powder
½ cup (60 g) ground almonds
2 eggs
8 ripe apricots, halved and pitted
2 tbsp. apricot jelly
2 tsp. water
¼ cup (30 g) sliced almonds, to decorate

1 Preheat the oven to 350°F (180°C, Gas 4). Grease a 9-in. (23-cm) cake pan and bottom-line with waxed paper.

2 Cream the butter or margarine with the sugar until pale and fluffy. Beat in the almond extract.

3 Mix the flour, baking powder, and ground almonds in a bowl. In a separate bowl, beat the eggs until they are pale and thick.

4 Fold the dry ingredients into the butter mixture alternately with the beaten eggs. Spoon the mixture into the prepared pan and arrange the apricots on top, rounded side up. Bake for 35 minutes.

5 Let the cake cool in the pan 10 minutes. Carefully remove the cake from the pan, lift off the paper, then place, with the apricot side uppermost, on a wire rack. Let cool another 10 minutes.

6 Melt the apricot jelly with the water in a small pan. Press the mixture through a strainer into a bowl. Brush the top of the cake with the apricot glaze and scatter the almonds on top. Serve in slices.

Swiss Roll with Lemon Cream

This family favorite can also be filled with jelly, buttercream, or cream and the fruit of your choice, but berries and soft fruit work particularly well.

Serves 6

4 large eggs
scant 1/2 cup (100 g) sugar
scant 1 cup (100 g) all-purpose flour

Filling
1 cup (225 g) mascarpone cheese
1 tsp. grated lemon peel
1 tbsp. fresh lemon juice
2 tbsp. fresh orange juice
1/4 cup (25 g) confectioners' sugar, plus extra for dusting

1 Preheat the oven to 425°F (220°C, Gas 7). Grease a 9 x 13-in. (23 x 33-cm) jelly roll pan and bottom-line with waxed paper.

2 Beat the eggs and sugar with a hand-held electric mixer in a large bowl until the mixture is thick and frothy and leaves a trail when lifted out of the bowl (ribbon stage).

3 Sift and fold in the flour in three batches with a large metal spoon. Pour the mixture into the prepared pan and spread into the corners. Bake until golden and the top springs back when pressed lightly, about 10 minutes.

4 While the cake is baking lay a sheet of waxed paper on a work surface and sprinkle liberally with a little of the extra confectioners' sugar.

5 Holding the lining paper and pan edges, turn the cake out onto the paper. Peel the lining paper from the cake. Trim off the edges and score a cut 1 inch (2.5 cm) in from one of the shorter ends.

6 Place a sheet of waxed paper over the surface and roll up from the scored end with the paper inside. Let cool on a wire rack.

7 To make the filling, beat all the ingredients together. Carefully unroll the cake, remove the paper, and spread the cake with the filling. Roll up, cut into slices, and serve.

Caribbean Banana Loaf

This recipe is a great way to use up overripe bananas that no one wants to eat—they are transformed into a deliciously moist and spicy cake.

Serves 6–8

2 bananas, peeled
2 tbsp. clear honey
1¾ cups (200 g) self-rising flour
½ tsp. baking powder
1 tsp. grated nutmeg
⅔ cup (150 g) butter, softened
¾ cup (150 g) packed light brown sugar
2 eggs, beaten
⅓ cup (50 g) pecans, finely chopped

1 Preheat the oven to 350°F (180°C, Gas 4). Grease an 8 x 4 x 3-in. (21 x 10 x 7.5-cm) loaf pan and bottom-line with waxed paper.

2 Mash the bananas with the honey. Sift the flour, baking powder, and nutmeg together in a separate bowl.

3 Cream the butter and sugar in a large mixing bowl until light and fluffy. Add the eggs a little at a time, beating well between additions.

4 Fold in the bananas and the flour mixture with the pecans. Spoon the mixture into the prepared loaf pan and bake until golden and a skewer inserted in the center comes out clean, 50 minutes to 1 hour.

5 Let cool in the pan for 10 minutes before turning out onto a wire rack to cool completely.

Fruit Tea Loaf

This recipe is incredibly easy to make, and the cake is a great standby in case family or friends visit. It's delicious served spread with butter.

Serves 6–8

2 cups (300 g) dried mixed fruit, such as
    golden raisins, currants, raisins, and
    candied cherries
generous ½ cup (125 g) packed light
    brown sugar
½ cup (120 g) butter
scant 1 cup (200 ml) brewed tea
2 tsp. ground allspice
finely grated peel of 1 orange
2 cups (225 g) self-rising flour, sifted

1 Place the dried mixed fruit, sugar, butter, tea, and allspice in a saucepan. Cover and heat gently over low heat until the butter has melted. Bring to a boil, cook 1 minute, then remove from the heat. Add the orange peel and let cool overnight.

2 Preheat the oven to 350°F (180°C, Gas 4). Grease and bottom-line a 28 x 4 x 3-in. (21 x 10 x 7.5-cm) loaf pan.

3 Fold the sifted flour into the fruit mixture. Pour the mixture into the prepared pan and bake until golden and a skewer inserted in the center comes out clean, 50 to 55 minutes.

4 Let cool in the pan, then turn out onto a wire rack. Serve in slices with butter, if desired.

"We cannot set aside an hour for discussion with our children and hope that it will be a time of deep encounter. The special moments of intimacy are more likely to happen while baking a cake together..."

Neil Kurshan

Cinnamon Swirl Teabread

Your reputation as a generous hostess will be greatly enhanced with this light, yeasty, spice-scented bread. It is similar to a brioche, which is why it needs extra yeast to help it rise. Serve with tea.

Serves 6–8

6½ cups (750 g) bread flour
½ cup (120 g) sugar
1 tsp. salt
2 tbsp. (25 g) fast-acting dried yeast
½ cup (120 g) unsalted butter
1⅔ cups (400 ml) milk
2 eggs, beaten
4 heaping tbsp. brown sugar
2 tsp. cinnamon

1 Place the flour, sugar, and salt in a large mixing bowl. Stir in the dried yeast. Make a well in the center of the flour.

2 Melt the butter in a saucepan. Pour in the milk and heat until it is just hand hot. Pour the mixture into the well in the flour, add the eggs and mix everything together with a wooden spoon until it forms a smooth, very soft dough.

3 Cover the dough and let rise in a warm place until doubled in size, 45 to 60 minutes. Mix the brown sugar with the cinnamon.

4 Beat the dough with a wooden spoon to deflate it. With well-floured hands, divide the dough into four pieces. Butter a nonstick 12-cup Bundt pan or a kugelhopf mold.

5 Preheat the oven to 425°F (220°C, Gas 7). Place a piece of dough in the mold and stretch it around the bottom until it is covered. Sprinkle with a quarter of the cinnamon-sugar mixture.

6 Take a second piece of dough and stretch it over the first one. Sprinkle with cinnamon sugar. Repeat twice more. Let rise 15 minutes.

7 Bake 20 minutes. Reduce the oven to 375°F (190°C, Gas 5) and bake the bread another 5 to 10 minutes. Turn out onto a wire rack and let cool.

Small
Cakes
&
Bars

Brunch Cupcakes

These little buns are perfect for a
quick breakfast because they are
packed full of high-energy ingredients
to help kick-start your day.
Alternatively, serve them drizzled with
a little frosting for afternoon tea.

Makes 12–14

1¼ cups (145 g) all-purpose flour
1 tbsp. baking powder
1 tsp. cinnamon
1/3 cup (50 g) ground toasted hazelnuts
1/4 cup (45 g) sugar
grated peel of 1 orange
1/3 cup (75 g) butter, melted
scant 1/2 cup (100 ml) milk
2 eggs, beaten
1 dessert apple, peeled, cored,
  and grated
3 tbsp. fresh orange juice
1/2 cup (60 g) coarsely chopped
  toasted hazelnuts

1 Preheat the oven to 400°F (200°C,
Gas 6). Line a muffin pan with paper
baking cups.

2 Sift the flour, baking powder, and
cinnamon together in a large mixing
bowl. Stir in the ground toasted hazelnuts
and sugar.

3 Mix the orange peel with the melted
butter, milk, and eggs. Stir the apple
into the flour mixture, then gently stir in
the egg and butter mixture with the
orange juice.

4 Spoon into the paper baking cups
and top each one with a few chopped
hazelnuts. Bake until well risen and
golden, 15 minutes. Turn out of the pan
and cool slightly on a wire rack before
serving.

Pineapple and Coconut Squares

The crushed pineapple helps to moisten this excellent coconut cake. It is served with a creamy topping, but would be equally delicious served warm with custard sauce or cream.

Serves 8–10

1 oz. (25 g) semolina flour
1 1/2 cups (175 g) all-purpose flour
1 tbsp. baking powder
1/4 cup (60 g) canned crushed pineapple in juice
2/3 cup (150 g) butter
2/3 cup (150 g) sugar
3 eggs, beaten
1/3 cup (50 g) shredded coconut

Topping
scant 1/2 cup (100 g) cream cheese, softened
1/3 cup (75 g) butter, softened
scant 1 cup (100 g) confectioners' sugar, sifted
1/2 tsp. vanilla extract
1 oz. (25 g) flaked coconut, toasted

1 Preheat the oven to 350°F (180°C, Gas 4). Grease and bottom-line an 11 x 7-in. (28 x 18-cm) cake pan.

2 Sift the semolina, flour, and baking powder together into a bowl. Put the pineapple into a strainer and let drain. Meanwhile, cream the butter and sugar together in a separate bowl until light and fluffy.

3 Beat in the eggs a little at a time, adding some flour if the mixture begins to separate. Fold in the flour mixture with the coconut and pineapple. Spoon the mixture into the prepared pan and spread over evenly.

4 Bake until risen, golden, and just firm to the touch, 35 to 40 minutes. Remove from the oven and let cool in the pan.

5 To make the topping, beat the cream cheese, butter, sugar, and vanilla together until smooth, light, and creamy. Spread over the top and sides of the cake and scatter the toasted coconut around the edges. Cut into squares or fingers to serve.

With its impressive crown of spiky leaves, **the pineapple is sometimes called the king of fruits.** Christopher Columbus brought it from South America, and it quickly became a matter of prestige for members of the European aristocracy to be able to say they had tasted this rare and unusual fruit.

Fruit Gingerbread

**Everyone will enjoy this afternoon
treat—it's really a cross between a
cake and a teabread, and it is delicious
served sliced with butter.**

Serves 6–8

3 1/2 cups (400 g) all-purpose flour
1 tsp. baking powder
1 tbsp. ground ginger
1 tsp. cinnamon
1 cup (225 g) unsalted butter
1/2 cup (125 g) dark molasses
3/4 cup (175 g) packed light brown sugar
3 eggs
3 oz. (75 g) dried cherries, halved
4 oz. (115 g) chopped dates
2 oz. (50 g) drained preserved ginger,
  chopped
3/4 cup (90 g) golden raisins

1 Preheat the oven to 300°F (150°C,
Gas 2). Grease and bottom-line an 8-in.
(21-cm) square cake pan.

2 Mix the flour, baking powder, ginger,
and cinnamon in a large bowl.

3 Place the butter in a saucepan with
the molasses and brown sugar and stir
over low heat until melted. Pour into the
flour mixture and mix well. Beat in the
eggs and stir in the remaining
ingredients.

4 Pour the mixture into the prepared
cake pan and bake until a skewer
inserted in the center comes out clean,
1 to 1 1/4 hours. Turn out onto a wire rack
and let cool.

THE HISTORY OF GINGERBREAD

Gingerbread, immortalized by the fairy tales of "The Gingerbread Man" and the gingerbread house in "Hansel and Gretel," is one of America's most popular cakes and a great Christmas tradition. Gingerbread has been baked across Europe for centuries. Almost every country and every family had its own variation of gingerbread, which was often cut into shapes, such as stars, hearts, animals, and men, depending on the occasion.

Germany has the strongest gingerbread-making tradition in the world. The Lebkuchler—the Guild of Master Bakers— in Nuremberg carved beautifully decorated and intricate gingerbread decorations to be sold at fairs and markets across the country. They are probably most famous for their Hexenhaeusle—witches' houses—which are based on the famous gingerbread house in the German fairy tale "Hansel and Gretel."

German settlers brought the tradition of making gingerbread with them to America, where local ingredients, such as maple syrup and molasses, produced a wider variety of gingerbread recipes. At Christmas, gingerbread makes a strong appearance in American homes, and the simple witches' houses now compete with even more spectacular gingerbread creations, including elaborate Victorian houses and miniature candy-covered villages!

Double Chocolate Chunk Brownies

It's important that brownies are not overcooked because they will lose their characteristic gooey center. Add any nuts you prefer, such as peanuts or macadamias, but in my mind, pecans go best of all with chocolate.

Makes 12

1¼ lb. (500 g) semisweet chocolate
1 cup (225 g) butter, diced
1 tsp. instant coffee powder
1 tbsp. hot water
3 large eggs
2/3 cup (150 g) sugar
1 tsp. vanilla extract
scant 1 cup (100 g) all-purpose flour
1 tsp. baking powder
1 cup (150 g) pecans, broken into pieces

1 Preheat the oven to 375°F (190°C, Gas 5). Grease an 8 x 12-in. (20 x 30-cm) cake pan and bottom-line with waxed paper.

2 Chop 6 oz. (175 g) of the chocolate into chunks and set aside. Break up the rest, put into a heatproof bowl with the butter, and melt slowly over a pan of simmering water. Stir until smooth, then let cool. Meanwhile, dissolve the coffee in the hot water.

3 Lightly beat together the eggs, coffee, sugar, and vanilla extract. Gradually beat in the chocolate and butter mixture, then fold in the flour, baking powder, pecans, and chocolate chunks. Pour into the prepared pan and bake until firm to the touch, 35 to 40 minutes.

4 Let cool for 5 minutes, then cut into squares. Let cool in the pan before removing the paper.

Pumpkin and Nut Muffins
with Brown Butter Frosting

Muffins are one of the most favorite small cakes, popular with adults and children alike. These are extra special, with their unusual pumpkin filling and delicious buttery frosting.

Makes 12

1/2 cup (120 g) butter, softened,
   plus extra for greasing
11/4 cups (145 g) all-purpose flour
3/4 cup (175 g) packed light brown sugar
8 oz. (225 g) canned or cooked pumpkin
1 large egg
2 tsp. cinnamon
1 tsp. vanilla extract
1 tsp. baking powder
1 tsp. baking soda
1/2 tsp. grated nutmeg
scant 3/4 cup (175 ml) milk
1 cup (120 g) whole wheat flour

2/3 cup (75 g) pecans, roughly chopped
3/4 cup (100 g) raisins

Frosting
1/4 cup (60 g) unsalted butter
13/4 cups (225 g) confectioners' sugar
11/2 tsp. vanilla extract
2 tbsp. milk

1 Preheat the oven to 375° F (190° C, Gas 5). Lightly grease a 12-cup muffin pan or line it with paper baking cups.

2 Cream the butter until fluffy using a hand-held electric mixer. Add the flour, sugar, pumpkin, egg, cinnamon, vanilla extract, baking powder, baking soda, nutmeg, and milk. Beat until well combined, scraping down the sides of the bowl occasionally.

3 Add the whole wheat flour, pecans, and raisins and fold in until just combined.

4 Fill the prepared pan until each cup is about two-thirds full. Transfer to the oven and bake until risen and golden, 25 to 30 minutes. Remove from the oven and let cool on a wire rack.

5 To make the frosting, melt the butter over medium heat in a small saucepan until light golden brown. Remove from the heat and immediately add the confectioners' sugar, vanilla extract, and milk, stirring until smooth. Spread generously over the top of each cooled muffin.

Chocolate Chip Muffins

These are a true classic. They are best eaten on the day of baking, which won't be difficult! Alternatively, they can be warmed for a few seconds in the microwave to freshen them up. Use the best quality chocolate for the most delicious results.

Makes 12

1 3/4 cups (200 g) all-purpose flour
1/2 cup (55 g) cocoa powder
1 oz. (25 g) semolina flour
1 tbsp. baking powder
1/3 cup (75 g) sugar
1 cup (250 ml) milk
3 eggs, beaten
scant 1/2 cup (100 g) butter, melted
3 1/2 oz. (90 g) semisweet chocolate,
 broken into small pieces

1 Preheat the oven to 400°F (200°C, Gas 6). Line a 12-cup muffin pan with paper baking cups.

2 Sift the flour, cocoa powder, semolina, and baking powder into a large bowl and stir in the sugar. Lightly beat together the milk, eggs, and butter, then gently fold into the flour.

3 Mix in the chocolate pieces—the mixture should be quite lumpy, so don't be tempted to beat it.

4 Spoon the mixture into the paper baking cups until they are three-quarters full and bake until well risen and golden, 20 to 25 minutes.

5 Remove the muffins from the pan and let cool slightly on a wire rack before serving.

Blueberry and White Chocolate Muffins

These muffins are delicious and are so easy to make. They are especially good served warm, so heat them gently in the microwave for a few seconds before serving.

Makes 12

2¹/₄ cups (250 g) all-purpose flour, sifted
¹/₃ cup (50 g) ground almonds
1 tbsp. baking powder
¹/₃ cup (75 g) sugar
1 cup (250 ml) milk
3 eggs, beaten
scant ¹/₂ cup (100 g) butter, melted
¹/₂ tsp. vanilla extract
5 oz. (150 g) blueberries
3 oz. (75 g) white chocolate,
   broken into small pieces

Topping
scant ¹/₂ cup (40 g) slivered almonds
2 tbsp. turbinado sugar

1 Preheat the oven to 400°F (200°C, Gas 6). Line a 12-cup muffin pan with paper baking cups.

2 Sift the flour, ground almonds, and baking powder into a large bowl and stir in the sugar. Lightly beat together the milk, eggs, and butter, then gently fold into the flour with the vanilla extract.

3 Mix in the blueberries and white chocolate pieces—the mixture should be quite lumpy so don't be tempted to beat it.

4 Spoon the mixture into the paper baking cups until they are three-quarters full. Top each one with a few almonds and a little turbinado sugar then bake until well risen and golden, 20 to 25 minutes.

5 Remove the muffins from the pan and let cool slightly on a wire rack before serving.

Peanut Butter Slices

It's important to use sugar-free peanut butter for these slices. You can use either smooth or crunchy varieties, but the crunchy does give an irresistible texture. These slices are great for picnics or packed lunches.

Makes 12

1³/4 cups (200 g) all-purpose flour
generous ¹/2 cup (85 g) whole wheat
  all-purpose flour
2 tsp. baking powder
generous 1 cup (225 g) packed light
  brown sugar
¹/2 cup (120 g) butter, softened
3 oz. (75 g) crunchy peanut butter
3 eggs, beaten
¹/3 cup (50 g) raisins

Topping

5 oz. (150 g) milk chocolate,
  broken into pieces
3¹/2 oz. (90 g) crunchy peanut butter
¹/2 cup (50 g) toasted slivered coconut,
  optional

1 Preheat the oven to 350°F (180°C, Gas 4). Grease an 11 x 7-in. (28 x 18-cm) cake pan and bottom-line with waxed paper.

2 Sift the flours and baking powder together into a bowl and beat in the sugar, butter, peanut butter, and eggs until smooth. Fold in the raisins, then spoon the mixture into the prepared pan and smooth evenly.

3 Bake until the edges are firm and the center is still slightly soft, 20 to 25 minutes. Transfer to a wire rack to cool.

4 To make the topping, melt the chocolate in a bowl set over a saucepan of simmering water. Stir in the peanut butter until melted, then spoon over the cake. Scatter the coconut over the top before cutting into bars.

THE PILLSBURY BAKE-OFF

In 1949, at the elegant Waldorf Astoria Hotel in New York, 100 amateur cooks shared their treasured recipes with the nation and competed in the first "Grand National Recipe and Baking Contest." The contest was held to celebrate Pillsbury's 80th anniversary and to promote Pillsbury Best Flour.

Mrs. Frank A. Greiner of Massachusetts (pictured) was one of the 100 finalists with her 80-minute biscuits, but the contest's first-ever winner was Mrs. Theodora Smafield of Michigan. Mrs. Smafield used a unique rising method to create her "No-Knead Water-Rising Twists" and was awarded $50,000 for her delicious and inventive recipe.

The event attracted thousands of entries and proved so popular that the company decided to hold it every year. The renamed "Bake-Off" continues to be as popular as ever and has become an American institution.

Applecake Bars

These applecake bars can be enjoyed with a cup of morning coffee or are just as delicious served as desserts with cream or custard sauce.

Serves 10–12

12 oz. (350 g) tart cooking apples, peeled, cored, and thinly sliced
juice of 1/2 lemon
scant 11/2 cups (325 g) butter
scant 11/2 cups (325 g) sugar
4 cups (450 g) all-purpose flour, sifted
3 tbsp. baking powder
11/2 tsp. cinnamon
grated peel of 1 lemon
6 eggs, beaten
3 tbsp. milk

Topping
2 tbsp. turbinado sugar
1/2 tsp. cinnamon
6 tbsp. apricot jelly or preserves, melted, to glaze

1 Preheat the oven to 350°F (180°C, Gas 4). Grease a 13 x 9 x 2-in. (33 x 23 x 5-cm) cake pan and bottom-line with waxed paper.

2 Toss the apple slices in the lemon juice. Cream the butter and sugar in a large mixing bowl until pale and fluffy. Sift in the flour, baking powder, and cinnamon. Add the lemon peel, eggs, and milk, and beat together until smooth.

3 Spoon half the mixture into the prepared pan. Top with half the apple slices, then the remaining cake mixture.

4 Arrange the remaining apple slices over the top and sprinkle with a mixture of turbinado sugar and cinnamon.

5 Bake until golden and firm to the touch, 50 to 60 minutes. Let cool in the pan 10 minutes then remove to a wire rack. Brush over the apricot jelly, then leave to cool completely. Cut into bars to serve.

Apples have been the world's favorite fruit for centuries. They were popular in ancient Greece and Rome, and there is even evidence that Stone Age man ate them centuries ago. Today there are over **7,000 apple varieties** worldwide and more than 40 million tons of apples are produced every year.

Frosted Lime Bars

**The crunchy topping is just as delicious
if you use lemon or orange juice in
place of lime. The secret is to pour it
over while the cake is still hot so the
juice soaks in and the sugar forms a
crunchy topping as it cools.**

Serves 6–8

1 cup (225 g) butter, softened
1 cup (225 g) sugar
2 cups (225 g) all-purpose flour
1 tbsp. baking powder
4 large eggs
2 tsp. grated lime peel

Topping
6 tbsp. fresh lime juice
4 tsp. grated lime peel
scant $1/2$ cup (100 g) sugar

1 Preheat the oven to 350°F (180°C,
Gas 4). Lightly grease a 7 x 11-in. (18 x
28-cm) cake pan and bottom-line with
waxed paper.

2 Place all the ingredients (except the
topping) in a bowl and beat until light
and smooth. Turn the mixture into the
prepared pan and spread out evenly.

3 Bake until the cake is well risen and
golden and the top springs back when
lightly pressed, 40 minutes.

4 While the cake is baking, mix the
topping ingredients together in a
small bowl. Remove the cake from the
oven and pour the topping over. Let
cool in the pan, then turn out and
remove the lining paper. Serve cut into
bars or squares.

Plum and Amaretti Sponge Slices

Crushed amaretti add an interesting crunch to these sponge slices, and the almond flavor works incredibly well with the plums. Serve with sour cream or vanilla ice cream.

Serves 6

3/4 cup (175 g) unsalted butter
3/4 cup (175 g) sugar
3 large eggs
1 1/2 cups (175 g) all-purpose flour, sifted
2 tsp. baking powder
2 tsp. grated lemon peel
1 tbsp. fresh lemon juice
3 plums, halved and pitted
1 oz. (25 g) amaretti cookies,
  coarsely crushed
1 tbsp. turbinado sugar, for sprinkling

1 Preheat the oven to 350°F (180°C, Gas 4). Grease a 7 x 11-in. (18 x 28-cm) cake pan and bottom-line with waxed paper.

2 Cream the butter and sugar together until pale and fluffy. Add the eggs a little at a time, whisking well after each addition. Sift the flour and baking powder together, then fold into the mixture with the lemon peel and juice.

3 Spoon into the prepared pan and spread into the corners. Arrange the plums, skin side up, on the top, then sprinkle with the amaretti and brown sugar. Bake until risen and golden, 45 to 50 minutes.

4 Remove from the pan and let cool on a wire rack before removing the lining paper. Cut into slices before serving.

Dessert Cakes

Strawberry Ice Cream Angel Cake

This ice cream-filled cake makes a dreamy dessert. Remove from the freezer 30 minutes before serving.

Serves 6–8

1/3 cup (55 g) all-purpose flour
2 tbsp. cornstarch
scant 1 cup (200 g) sugar
7 large egg whites
3/4 tsp. cream of tartar
pinch of salt
11/2 tsp. vanilla extract

Filling
1/4 cup (60 g) strawberry jelly
1 pint (450 g) strawberry ice cream
fresh strawberries, to serve

1 Preheat the oven to 350°F (180°C, Gas 4). Grease and bottom-line a 9-in. (23-cm) springform pan.

2 Sift the flour and cornstarch together. Add just under half of the sugar and sift together twice.

3 Beat the egg whites until foamy. Add the cream of tartar and salt, and continue whisking until they form stiff peaks.

4 Beat the remaining sugar into the egg whites until stiff and glossy. Beat in the vanilla extract.

5 Fold in the flour in three batches, then spoon into the prepared pan. The mixture should come up to the top. Smooth the top and bake until lightly golden and spongy to the touch, 45 to 50 minutes. Remove from the oven and invert onto a wire rack. Let cool in the pan.

6 Remove the cake from the pan. Wash and dry the pan and line with waxed paper. Cut the cake through horizontally and return the base to the pan.

7 Spread the jelly over the base and top with ice cream, spreading over evenly. Top with the other cake half and press down lightly. Freeze until firm. Serve topped with fresh strawberries.

Chocolate and Raspberry Torte

This elegant gateau with its delightful orange liqueur filling makes a fantastic dinner party dessert, especially when made with fresh raspberries. It can also be prepared ahead of time and frozen to save time on the day.

Serves 6–8

$1/3$ cup (55 g) all-purpose flour, sifted
$1/4$ cup (30 g) cocoa powder, sifted, plus extra for dusting
3 tbsp. unsalted butter
3 large eggs
$1/3$ cup (75 g) sugar

Filling
scant 2 cups (425 ml) heavy cream
$1/4$ cup (60 ml) orange liqueur
6 oz. (175 g) fresh or frozen raspberries
1 tbsp. confectioners' sugar
2 oz. (50g) bittersweet chocolate, at least 50% cocoa solids, grated

1 Preheat the oven to 350°F (180°C, Gas 4). Grease and bottom-line a 9-in. (23-cm) cake pan. Sift the flour and cocoa together and melt the butter.

2 Break the eggs into a large heatproof bowl and add the sugar. Place the bowl over a saucepan of simmering water and whisk until mixture leaves a trail when lifted out of the bowl (ribbon stage). Remove from the heat.

3 Add the sifted flour and cocoa in three batches, drizzling a little butter around the bowl between batches, and folding in. Leave any white sediment at the bottom of the saucepan.

4 Pour the mixture into the prepared pan and bake until golden and the top springs back when pressed lightly, 20 minutes. Let cool 2 to 3 minutes in the pan, then turn out onto a wire rack to cool completely.

5 To make the filling, whip the cream and orange liqueur until it forms soft peaks. Fold in the raspberries, sugar, and grated chocolate.

6 Slice the cake horizontally to make two layers. Line an 8-in. (20-cm) springform pan with waxed paper and trim the cake to fit the base of the pan.

7 Put one of the sponge cake halves at the bottom. Pile in the raspberry cream and top with the remaining cake half. Press down evenly and freeze 4 hours until the filling is firm.

8 Dust the top with cocoa, then remove from the pan and serve in slices.

According to Greek mythology, raspberries were originally white until the nymph Ida was scratched by the plant's thorns while picking berries to stop the young god Zeus from crying. The color of her blood turned the berries red, and they have remained that color ever since.

Chocolate and Chestnut Macaroon Cake

Drizzle this delicious layer cake with melted chocolate for a special finish.

Serves 6–8

2 cups (240 g) confectioners' sugar
1/2 tsp. baking soda
4 large egg whites
generous 1 cup (120 g) ground almonds

Filling
scant 1/2 cup (100 g) chestnut purée
2 tbsp. maple syrup
3 oz. (75 g) bittersweet chocolate, broken into pieces
1 cup (225 g) mascarpone cheese
1/2 cup (125 ml) heavy cream, whipped
chocolate curls, to decorate

1 Preheat the oven to 275°F (140°C, Gas 1). Line three baking sheets with waxed paper and draw a 7-in. (18-cm) circle on each.

2 Sift the confectioners' sugar and baking soda together. Beat the egg whites until they form stiff peaks.

3 Gradually whisk in three-quarters of the confectioners' sugar until stiff and glossy. Mix the remaining sugar into the ground almonds and fold into the whites.

4 Divide the mixture among the three circles and spread out evenly. Bake for 10 minutes. Reduce the oven temperature to 225°F (110°C, Gas 1/4) and bake an additional 11/4 hours. Let cool on a wire rack, then peel away the paper.

5 For the filling, beat the chestnut purée and maple syrup together until smooth. Melt the chocolate in a bowl over a pan of simmering water, then stir it into the chestnut purée. Beat in the mascarpone and fold in the cream.

6 Place a meringue circle on a plate and spread with half of the chestnut mixture. Place a second meringue on top and spread with the rest of the mixture. Top with the remaining meringue round. Decorate with chocolate curls.

Upside-Down Kumquat Cake

Some people know this as topsy-turvy cake, but whatever you call it, it's a real family favorite. To intensify the orange flavor, stir in 2 tbsp. orange marmalade. Sliced fresh peaches or nectarines also work well, or you could use drained canned fruit, such as pineapple rings.

Serves 6–8

1/2 cup (175 g) butter
6 oz. (175 g) kumquats
1/4 cup (60 g) packed light brown sugar
1/2 cup (120 g) sugar
1 cup (120 g) all-purpose flour
1 tsp. baking powder
1/4 tsp. salt
2 eggs, beaten
1/2 tsp. vanilla extract
cream or ice cream, to serve

1 Preheat the oven to 350°F (180°C, Gas 4). Melt half of the butter in the bottom of an 8-in. (20-cm) square cake pan. Dip a pastry brush in the butter and lightly grease the sides of the pan.

2 Bring a small pan of water to a boil, add the kumquats and cook 10 minutes. Drain well. When cool enough to handle, cut the kumquats in half lengthwise, scoop out and discard the seeds.

3 Sprinkle the brown sugar evenly over the bottom of the greased pan. Arrange the kumquat halves, cut side down, over the brown sugar.

4 Cream the remaining butter and sugar together in a bowl. Add the flour, baking powder, and salt alternately with the eggs. Beat in the vanilla extract.

5 Drop the mixture by spoonfuls into the pan, then gently level the top, taking care not to disturb the kumquats. Bake in the center of the oven until a skewer inserted in the center comes out clean, 30 to 35 minutes.

6 Let the cake cool in the pan 5 minutes, then invert on a plate. Serve warm with cream or ice cream.

Hazelnut Meringue Cake

This rich yet light hazelnut meringue filled with a bourbon-laced cream and fresh raspberries makes an impressive dinner party dessert. Fill the meringue about an hour before serving—any longer and it will start to go soft.

Serves 6–8

4 egg whites
scant 1 cup (200 g) sugar
1 tsp. vanilla extract
1 tsp. cider vinegar
1 tsp. cornstarch
2/3 cup (80 g) finely ground toasted hazelnuts
2 tbsp. coarsely chopped toasted hazelnuts

Filling
2/3 cup (75 g) plain yogurt
2 tbsp. bourbon
2 tbsp. honey
1/2 cup (125 ml) heavy cream
8 oz. (225 g) raspberries
confectioners' sugar, for dusting

1 Preheat the oven to 350°F (180°C, Gas 4). Grease two 8-in. (20-cm) round cake pans and bottom-line with waxed paper.

2 Beat the egg whites until they form stiff peaks. Gradually beat in the sugar to make a stiff and glossy meringue. Fold in the vanilla extract, vinegar, cornstarch, and ground hazelnuts.

3 Divide the mixture between the two prepared pans and spread evenly. Scatter the chopped hazelnuts over the top of one, then bake until crisp, 50 to 60 minutes. Turn out of the pans and let cool on a wire rack.

4 For the filling, stir the yogurt, bourbon, and honey together. Whip the cream until it forms soft peaks, then fold into the yogurt mixture with the raspberries.

5 Sandwich the two meringues together with the cream, with the nut-topped one uppermost. Dust with confectioners' sugar before serving.

Summer Fruit Roulade

The featherlight sponge cake encases sumptuous summer fruits and kirsch-flavored whipped cream.

Serves 6–8

5 large eggs, separated
generous 1/2 cup (140 g) sugar
3 oz. (75 g) creamed coconut, grated
confectioners' sugar, for dusting

Filling
8 oz. (225 g) mixed frozen summer fruits
1 tbsp. fresh orange juice
2 tsp. cornstarch
1/2 cup (125 ml) heavy cream
2 tsp. kirsch
2 tbsp. flaked coconut

1 Preheat the oven to 350°F (180°C, Gas 4). Grease a 9 x 13-in. (23 x 33-cm) jelly roll pan and bottom-line with waxed paper.

2 Beat the egg yolks and sugar until thick and glossy. In a separate bowl, beat the egg whites until they form stiff peaks.

3 Fold the creamed coconut into the egg yolk mixture. Gently stir in half the egg whites, then fold in the rest. Pour the mixture into the prepared pan.

4 Bake until risen and firm to the touch, about 20 minutes. Let cool in the pan, covered with a wire rack and a clean damp dish towel.

5 To make the filling, cook the fruit in a saucepan with the orange juice until the juices begin to run. Blend the cornstarch with a little water and stir into the fruit. Cook until thickened, then remove from the heat and set aside to cool. Whip the cream and kirsch together until it forms soft peaks.

6 Liberally dust a piece of waxed paper with confectioners' sugar, then turn the roulade out onto it. Peel off the paper. Spread the cake with the whipped cream and then the fruit.

7 Using the paper underneath to help, roll the roulade from one of the long sides. Transfer to a plate while still wrapped in the rolling paper.

8 Remove the paper and top with flaked coconut. Sift confectioners' sugar on top. Cut into slices and serve with extra whipped cream, if desired.

THE PILLSBURY BAKE-OFFS OF THE 1950s

In the 1950s, the Bake-Off began to change and a new junior division gave children the chance to compete for the first time. The first junior winner was Ruth Derousseau of Wisconsin with her recipe for "Cherry Winks."

The recipes in the Bake-Offs reflected the trends in cooking and family life in the 1950s. The predominance of sumptuous cakes and desserts showed an attitude of "the fancier, the better" and mirrored the wealth and abundance of the postwar years. Homemakers were enjoying new developments and appliances in the kitchen.

In the decades that followed, the contest continued to illustrate changes in the home—time-saving recipes were popular in the '60s, a new international flavor was evident in the '70s, and the '80s and '90s featured more health-conscious recipes and more male competitors. The Pillsbury Bake-Off continues to mirror and set trends in baking today and plays an important role in the history of American cooking.

Coconut and Cherry Jelly Roll

The kirsch-flavored cream filling and whole cherries raise this simple jelly roll to sumptuous dessert status. The creamed coconut has a lovely flavor and is less granular than the shredded sort.

Serves 6–8

4 large eggs
scant $1/2$ cup (100 g) sugar
scant 1 cup (100 g) all-purpose flour
2 oz. (50 g) creamed coconut,
  finely grated
confectioners' sugar, for dusting

Filling
$2/3$ cup (150 ml) heavy cream
2 tbsp. kirsch
8 oz. (225 g) pitted canned cherries,
  drained (or fresh when in season)

1 Preheat the oven to 425°F (220°C, Gas 7). Grease a 9 x 13-in. (23 x 33-cm) jelly roll pan and bottom-line with waxed paper.

2 Whisk the eggs and sugar with a hand-held electric mixer in a large bowl until the mixture is thick and frothy and leaves a trail when lifted out of the bowl (ribbon stage).

3 Add the sifted flour in three batches and fold in gently after each addition with a large metal spoon. Fold in the creamed coconut with the last batch of flour.

4 Pour into the prepared pan and spread lightly into the corners. Bake until golden and the top springs back when pressed, 10 minutes.

5 While the cake is baking lay a sheet of waxed paper on a work surface and sprinkle liberally with confectioners' sugar.

6 Holding the lining paper and pan edges, turn the cake out onto the paper. Peel the lining paper from the cake and trim the edges. Score a cut 1 inch (2.5 cm) in from one of the shorter ends.

7 Place a sheet of waxed paper over the surface and roll up from scored end with the paper inside. Let cool on a wire rack.

8 To make the filling, whip the cream and kirsch together until they form soft peaks. Unroll the cake, remove the paper, and fill with cream and cherries. Roll up and serve sliced.

The National Cherry Festival has been held in Traverse City, Michigan—the "Cherry Capital of the World"—since 1926. Thousands of visitors come from all over the world to join the locals in their weeklong celebration of the cherry harvest. Events range from the Taste of Cherries Cook-Off and guided tours of the orchards to music and sporting events, and even a cherry pit spitting contest!

Blueberry and White Chocolate Meringue Roll

This is a rather unusual dessert, since it uses a meringue mixture to create a type of roulade. The white chocolate cream filling is complemented by tangy, fragrant blueberries.

Serves 6

1/2 vanilla bean
1 cup (225 g) sugar
5 egg whites
confectioners' sugar, for dusting

Filling

5 oz. (150 g) white chocolate, broken
  into pieces
1/2 cup (115 g) plain yogurt
1 cup (225 g) mascarpone cheese
4 oz. (115 g) blueberries

1 Preheat the oven to 425°F (220°C, Gas 7). Grease a 9 x 13-in. (23 x 33-cm) jelly roll pan and bottom-line with waxed paper.

2 Split the vanilla bean and scrape out the seeds. Combine them with the sugar.

Beat the egg whites until they form stiff peaks. Gradually beat in the vanilla sugar to make a stiff and glossy meringue.

3 Spread the meringue mixture into the prepared pan and bake 8 minutes. Reduce the oven to 325°F (160°C, Gas 3) and continue baking until the meringue is firm to the touch, 10 minutes.

4 Remove the meringue from the oven and turn out onto a sheet of waxed paper dusted with confectioners' sugar. Remove the paper from the base and let cool, about 10 minutes.

5 Meanwhile, make the filling. Melt the chocolate in a heatproof bowl set over a saucepan of simmering water. Stir in the yogurt, then beat the mixture into the mascarpone. Spread the cream filling over the meringue and top with the blueberries. Roll up from one of the long sides using the paper underneath to help. Leave wrapped in the paper at least 1 hour before serving.

White Chocolate Cheesecake

This quick and easy, but no less delicious cheesecake does not require cooking, making it the perfect finale to any elegant dinner party.

Serves 10

6 oz. (175 g) ginger cookies
2 oz. (50 g) unsalted butter, melted
1 lb. (450 g) cream cheese, softened
2 eggs, separated
1 tsp. vanilla extract
1 tbsp. sugar
3 oz. (75 g) white chocolate chips
10 oz. (275 g) white chocolate, broken into pieces
2/3 cup (150 ml) heavy cream
seasonal soft fruit, to decorate

1 Place the ginger cookies in a food processor and process until they resemble fine bread crumbs. Transfer to a bowl and stir in the melted butter. Press the mixture into the base of an 8-in. (20-cm) springform pan and chill 15 minutes until firm.

2 Beat the cream cheese with the egg yolks, vanilla extract, and sugar. Stir in the chocolate chips.

3 Melt the chocolate in a heatproof bowl set over a pan of simmering water. Set aside to cool slightly, then carefully stir it into the cream cheese mixture and mix well.

4 Lightly whip the cream and fold into the chocolate mixture. Beat the egg whites until they form soft peaks and fold into the mixture.

5 Pour the mixture into the pan, smooth the surface, and let chill until set, 2 hours. Decorate with seasonal soft fruits.

Coffee Cheesecake with Pecan Sauce

Have guests purring with pleasure with this rich, creamy cheesecake made extra special with a luscious sauce.

Serves 6

7 oz. (200 g) graham crackers
1/4 cup (60 g) unsalted butter, melted
2 3/4 cups (600 g) cream cheese
1 cup (200 g) packed light brown sugar
1 tsp. vanilla extract
3 eggs
2 tbsp. very strong brewed coffee

Sauce
4 tbsp. unsalted butter
6 tbsp. soft light brown sugar
1 cup (250 ml) heavy cream
1 tsp. vanilla extract
3/4 cup (75 g) pecans, toasted and finely chopped

1 Preheat the oven to 350°F (180°C, Gas 4).

2 Crush the crackers into fine crumbs and stir in the melted butter. Press into the bottom of an 8-in. (20-cm) springform pan and chill 20 minutes.

3 Beat the cream cheese with the sugar and vanilla extract. Add the eggs and beat until smooth. Stir in the coffee, then spoon the mixture into the pan.

4 Wrap the base and sides of the pan with aluminum foil, then place it in a roasting pan half full of boiling water and bake 55 minutes. Turn off the heat and let the cheesecake cool in the oven about 1 hour. Chill for at least 1 hour in the refrigerator before serving.

5 To make the sauce, melt the butter in a small saucepan and add the sugar, cream, and vanilla extract. Simmer 10 minutes, then stir in the pecans. Serve warm with the cold cheesecake.

Classic Cheesecake with Blackberry Topping

You can't beat a classic baked cheesecake. This lemon version is topped with a blackberry glaze, but it is just as delicious pure and simple without any topping at all. Alternatively, top with any soft berries of your choice—raspberry and strawberry glazes are especially good.

Serves 6–8

14 graham crackers
5 tbsp. butter, melted
3 large eggs, separated
3/4 cup (175 g) sugar
11/2 cups (350 g) cream cheese, softened
3/4 cup (185 ml) sour cream
2 tbsp. cornstarch
2 tsp. vanilla extract
4 tsp. grated lemon peel

Topping
1 lb. (450 g) blackberries
1/4 cup (60 ml) water
scant 1/2 cup (100 g) sugar
4 tsp. arrowroot
1/4 cup (60 ml) blackberry or cherry liqueur

1 Preheat the oven to 350°F (180°C, Gas 4). Grease and bottom-line a 9-in. (23-cm) springform pan. Mix the crackers and butter together and press into the base of the pan.

2 Beat the egg yolks and half the sugar until light and fluffy. Add the cream cheese a little at a time, whisking until smooth. Mix in the sour cream, cornstarch, vanilla extract, lemon peel, and the remaining sugar.

3 In a separate bowl, beat the egg whites until they form stiff peaks, then fold them into the mixture. Pour into the prepared pan.

4 Bake until just set and golden on top, 1 to 1 1/4 hours. Run a knife around the inside of the pan, then let cool in the oven with the door ajar.

5 Meanwhile, make the topping. Cook the blackberries, water, and sugar until the juices run and the berries are soft, 5 minutes. Blend the arrowroot with the liqueur and stir into the fruit. Bring to a boil, then remove from the heat and set aside to cool.

6 Remove the cheesecake from the pan. Pour the blackberry glaze over the top. Chill 4 hours before serving.

CHEESECAKE AND THE GREAT AMERICAN DINER

One of our most popular and versatile desserts and a must on every diner's menu is the cheesecake. Although it is considered an American classic, the humble cheesecake has existed across Western Europe in one form or another for centuries. The Romans spread their pastry version of the original Greek dish across Europe, and it was even served to athletes at the first ever Olympic Games in 776 B.C.

The most popular cheesecake since the invention of cream cheese is the classic New York cheesecake—with its pure creamy filling and graham-cracker crust, it is still a real American favorite. No one knows who first made the dessert in this style, but many believe that cheesecake simply wasn't cheesecake until it was made in New York!

From an elegant hotel or trendy bistro to the roughest truck-stop diner—wherever you can buy dessert, you can buy cheesecake. It is the quintessential American dessert, and the possibility of a New York diner not serving at least one kind of cheesecake is inconceivable!

Banana Toffee Cheesecake

**A deliciously gooey and indulgent
cheesecake with a fresh banana filling.**

Serves 10–12

2 cups (225 g) all-purpose flour
pinch of salt
1/2 cup (120 g) cold butter, diced
1/4 cup (55 g) sugar
3–4 tbsp. cold water

Filling
4 oz. (115 g) semisweet chocolate,
    broken into pieces, plus extra
    to decorate
14-oz. (400-g) can sweetened
    condensed milk
3 large ripe but firm bananas, sliced
juice of 1/2 lemon
generous 1 cup (250 g) mascarpone
    cheese
2/3 cup (150 ml) heavy cream, lightly
    whipped

1 Sift the flour into a mixing bowl with
the salt. Add the butter and, using your
fingertips, rub or cut the butter into the
flour until the mixture resembles coarse
bread crumbs. Mix in the sugar.

2 Add the cold water and, using your
hands or a narrow spatula, start to bring
the dough together, adding a little more
water, if necessary. Knead the dough into
a ball, cover with plastic wrap and chill
30 minutes.

3 Preheat the oven to 400°F (200°C,
Gas 6).

4 Roll out the pastry on a lightly floured
surface into a large circle, about 2 in.
(5 cm) larger than a 9-in. (23-cm) tart
pan, and place on waxed paper. Ease the
pastry into the pan. Line the pie shell
with waxed paper and baking beans.

5 Bake the pie shell about 12 minutes. Remove the baking beans and paper and bake until golden, 10 to 12 minutes. Set aside to cool. Brush off any crumbs from inside the shell.

6 To make the filling, melt the chocolate in a bowl set over a saucepan of simmering water. Do not let the bowl touch the water. Using a pastry brush, paint the chocolate onto the pie shell to cover completely. Chill until set.

7 Put the can of condensed milk into a deep pan and cover with water by at least 2 in. (5 cm). Bring to a boil and simmer 4 hours, topping up with water as necessary. Keep the can completely submerged at all times. Remove the pan from the heat and let the can stand until completely cold before opening.

8 To assemble the cheesecake, drizzle the sliced bananas with lemon juice. Beat the mascarpone cheese until softened, then stir in the cream. Carefully fold the cream mixture and condensed milk together, but don't overmix—leave them marbled. Fold in the bananas, then spoon into the pastry shell. Grate the extra chocolate over the top.

The banana is believed by some horticulturists to be the world's first fruit, and history records Alexander the Great discovering them in India as long ago as 327 B.C. However, the fruit was not officially introduced into America until the Philadelphia Centennial Exhibition of 1876, and the first commercial shipment of bananas did not reach Britain until 1902.

Celebration
Cakes

Festive Chocolate and Hazelnut Roulade

This special dessert is really easy and can even be made the day before the celebration. If serving at Christmas, decorate with chocolate holly leaves before dusting with extra confectioners' sugar.

Serves 6–8

6 oz. (175 g) bittersweet chocolate, at least 50% cocoa solids, broken into pieces
6 eggs, separated
2/3 cup (150 g) sugar
1/2 cup (60 g) ground hazelnuts
confectioners' sugar, for dusting

Filling
1 cup (250 ml) heavy cream
1 tbsp. brandy

1 Preheat the oven to 350°F (180°C, Gas 4). Grease a 9 x 13-in. (23 x 33-cm) jelly roll pan and bottom-line with waxed paper.

2 Melt the chocolate in a heatproof bowl set over a saucepan of simmering water. Set aside to cool slightly.

3 Beat the egg yolks and sugar until thick, smooth, and glossy. In a separate bowl, beat the egg whites until they form stiff peaks.

4 Fold the cooled chocolate and the ground hazelnuts into the egg yolk mixture. Gently stir in half the egg whites, then fold in the rest.

5 Pour the mixture into the prepared pan and bake until risen and firm to the touch, 20 minutes.

6 Let cool in a pan, covered with a wire rack and a clean, damp dish towel.

7 Whip the cream and brandy together until it forms soft peaks. Liberally dust a piece of waxed paper with confectioners' sugar, then turn the roulade out onto it.

8 Peel off the lining paper and spread with the cream. Use the paper to help you roll the roulade from one long side.

9 Transfer to a plate while still wrapped in the rolling paper. Remove the paper and sift extra sugar over, if liked. Cut into slices and serve with extra whipped cream, if desired.

Baked Alaska Birthday Cake

Dim the lights and light the candles; it's time to sing "Happy Birthday." This cake is an all-time favorite, but the fresh raspberries make it really special.

Serves 6–8

3/4 cup (175 g) unsalted butter
3/4 cup (175 g) sugar
3 eggs, beaten
1 tsp. vanilla extract
1 1/2 cups (175 g) all-purpose flour, sifted
2 tsp. baking powder
12 oz. (350 g) raspberry jelly
8 oz. (225 g) raspberries
4 egg whites
1 cup (225 g) sugar
8 scoops vanilla ice cream, or your
    favorite flavor
candles or sparklers, to decorate

1 Preheat the oven to 350°F (180°C, Gas 4). Grease and bottom-line an 8-in. (20-cm) cake pan.

2 Cream the butter and sugar in a large bowl until pale and fluffy. Add the eggs

and vanilla extract and beat well. Sift the flour and baking powder together, then fold into the mixture. Pour the mixture into the prepared pan. Smooth the top and bake until risen and golden, 30 to 35 minutes. Turn out and cool on a wire rack.

3 Split the cake in half horizontally. Place the bottom half on a baking sheet and spread with the raspberry jelly. Place the second cake disk on top. Arrange the raspberries on top of the cake.

4 Place the egg whites in a large bowl and beat until they form stiff peaks. Beat in the sugar a spoonful at a time. Turn up the oven to 425°F (220°C, Gas 7).

5 Place scoops of ice cream over the raspberries to cover. Spread the meringue mixture over the ice cream and the sides of the cake so everything is covered. Bake for 8 to 10 minutes.

6 Decorate the cake with birthday candles and serve immediately.

BIRTHDAY CAKE TRADITIONS

Birthdays are celebrated around the world in many different ways, but the birthday cake is one of the oldest traditions. Historians are unsure when the custom began, but they know the ancient Greeks baked honey cakes to celebrate the birthdays of their gods. There is even evidence suggesting candles were put on the cakes presented to Artemis, the goddess of the moon and the hunt, to symbolize moonlight.

The birthday cake tradition reappeared in the 13th century at German Kinderfeste celebrations, at which young children were awoken on their birthdays with cakes topped with lighted candles. This celebration marked the beginning of children's birthday parties and established the tradition that children's wishes would come true if they blew out all their birthday candles in one breath.

In Sweden today, birthday cakes are similar to pound cakes and are covered with marzipan, but in Russia children are presented with birthday pies, not cakes. In America and Britain, most families continue to celebrate with cakes covered in candles and by singing "Happy Birthday." This tradition has now spread to many other countries, including Panama, Uruguay, New Zealand, and the Philippines, and is continuing to become more and more popular throughout the world.

"…**I remembered that dear grandma always made you a little cake like that, and that you once said it wouldn't be a happy birthday without it.**"

Louisa May Alcott

American Whipped Sponge Cake

This traditional American, light-as-a-feather sponge cake is flavored with vanilla and is great for any special occasion when filled with fresh fruit and cream.

Serves 6–8

3 large eggs, separated
scant 1/2 cup (100 g) sugar
1 tsp. vanilla extract
1/4 tsp. cream of tartar
1/3 cup (55 g) all-purpose flour, sifted
pinch of salt

Filling
1 cup (250 ml) heavy cream
4 oz. (115 g) strawberries, halved if large
confectioners' sugar, for dusting

1 Preheat the oven to 350°F (180°C, Gas 4). Grease and bottom-line an 8-in (20-cm) springform pan.

2 Beat the egg yolks with half of the sugar until thick and pale. Beat in the vanilla extract.

3 Beat the egg whites and cream of tartar until they form stiff peaks. Gradually beat in the remaining sugar until stiff and glossy. Fold in the sifted flour and salt with a quarter of the whisked egg whites. Fold in the remaining egg whites.

4 Spoon the mixture into the prepared pan and bake until golden and the top springs back when pressed lightly, 30 to 40 minutes.

5 Turn the cake upside down on a wire rack and let cool 30 minutes in the pan. Run a knife around the inside of the pan, then turn the cake out onto the wire rack. Turn right side up and let cool completely.

6 Whip the cream to soft peaks and pile onto the cake. Spread over the top and sides and decorate with small whole or halved strawberries. Dust the top with confectioners' sugar before serving.

Passion Cake

This deliciously moist carrot cake is a traditional British dessert. It has a thick, indulgent layer of sweet cream cheese icing on top, making it all the more special. Walnuts can be substituted for the pecans, if preferred.

Serves 6–8

2/3 cup (150 ml) sunflower oil
3/4 cup (150 g) packed light brown sugar
3 eggs, beaten
1/2 tsp. cinnamon
1/2 tsp. grated nutmeg
5 oz. (150 g) carrots, coarsely grated
1 banana, mashed
1/3 cup (50 g) pecans, chopped
2 1/4 cups (250 g) all-purpose flour, sifted
1 tbsp. baking powder

Topping
2/3 cup (160 g) cream cheese, softened
scant 1 cup (100 g) confectioners' sugar, sifted
grated peel of 1/2 orange
1/4 cup (50 g) chopped pecans

1 Preheat the oven to 350°F (180°C, Gas 4). Grease and bottom-line an 8-in. (20-cm) square pan.

2 Put all the cake ingredients into a large mixing bowl and beat together well.

3 Spoon the mixture into the prepared pan, spread evenly, and bake until golden and a skewer inserted in the center comes out clean, 45 to 50 minutes.

4 Let cool in the pan 10 minutes, then turn out onto a wire rack to cool completely.

5 To make the topping, beat the cream cheese, sugar, and orange peel together until light and fluffy. Spread over the top of the cake and scatter with pecans before serving.

Walnut and Strawberry Celebration Cake

This makes a wonderful cake to serve at any special celebration. Layers of moist walnut cake are sandwiched together with fresh strawberries and a deliciously sweet frosting for a really luxurious confection.

Serves 6–8

1/3 cup (50 g) walnuts
4 eggs, beaten
scant 1/2 cup (100 g) sugar
1/2 cup (75 g) all-purpose flour, sifted
1 tsp. baking powder
1/3 cup (50 g) walnuts, finely chopped, to decorate

Frosting
1 egg white
3/4 cup (175 g) sugar
1 tbsp water
a few drops of rosewater
7 oz. (200 g) small strawberries, hulled

1 Preheat the oven to 350°F (180°C, Gas 4). Grease an 8-in (20-cm) springform pan and bottom-line with waxed paper.

2 Grind the walnuts in a food processor until finely chopped—don't overprocess or the nuts will become oily.

3 Beat the eggs and sugar together in a large mixing bowl set over a saucepan of simmering water until thick and frothy and the mixture leaves a trail when lifted out of the bowl (ribbon stage). Remove from the heat.

4 Sift the flour and walnuts over the egg mixture and fold in gently. Pour into the prepared cake pan and bake until well risen, golden, and just firm to the touch, 40 to 45 minutes. Let cool in the pan 5 minutes, then transfer to a wire rack to cool completely.

5 To make the frosting, put all the ingredients in a large mixing bowl set over a saucepan of simmering water. Beat with a hand-held electric mixer until thick, 10 to 12 minutes.

6 Up to 4 hours before serving, slice the cake through horizontally to make two layers. Sandwich them together with a little frosting and some sliced strawberries, reserving a few to decorate.

7 Use the remaining frosting to spread over the top and sides of the cake. Halve the rest of the strawberries and arrange them on top of the cake to decorate.

8 To finish, press the chopped walnuts into the sides of the cake using a narrow spatula or palette knife.

Middle Eastern Orange Cake

The whole orange, including the pith and peel, gives this moist and delicious cake a really intense citrus flavor. Serve with sour cream or whipped cream at a birthday lunch or as a wonderful Mother's Day treat.

Serves 8–10

2 small oranges
5 eggs
scant 1 cup (175 g) packed light
   brown sugar
generous 1 1/2 cups (225 g) ground
   almonds
1/3 cup (55 g) all-purpose flour
1 tsp. baking powder
2 tbsp. slivered almonds
confectioners' sugar, for dusting
whipped cream, to serve

1 Put the oranges in a saucepan and cover with water. Bring to a boil, cover, and simmer until the oranges are very soft, about 1 1/2 hours. Drain and let cool. Halve the oranges and remove the pips then purée in a food processor or electric blender. Measure 1 1/4 cups (300 ml) of the pulp and discard the rest.

2 Preheat the oven to 350°F (180°C, Gas 4). Grease and bottom-line a 9-in. (23-cm) cake pan.

3 Beat the eggs and sugar with a hand-held electric mixer in a large bowl until thick and frothy, and the mixture leaves a trail when lifted out of the bowl (ribbon stage).

4 Fold the orange pulp into the egg mixture with the almonds, flour, and baking powder. Pour the mixture into the prepared pan, scatter the slivered almonds over the surface, and bake 1 hour or until a skewer inserted in the center comes out clean.

5 Let cool 10 minutes, then remove from the pan and peel off the lining paper. Dust the top with confectioners' sugar. Let cool on a wire rack or serve warm with whipped cream.

Devil's Food Cake
with Chocolate Orange frosting

This is a chocoholic's dream—wickedly indulgent, rich, and delicious with a tempting layer of chocolate orange frosting. Who could resist?

Serves 8

6 oz. (175 g) bittersweet chocolate, broken into pieces
2/3 cup (150 g) unsalted butter
2/3 cup (150 g) sugar
6 large eggs, separated
1/2 cup (75 g) all-purpose flour
1/3 cup (40 g) ground almonds

Frosting
3/4 cup (185 ml) heavy cream
7 oz. (200 g) bittersweet chocolate, broken into pieces
2 tsp. grated orange peel
confectioners' sugar, for dusting

1 Preheat the oven to 350°F (180°C, Gas 4). Grease an 8-in. (20-cm) cake pan and bottom-line with waxed paper.

2 Melt the chocolate in a heatproof bowl set over a pan of simmering water. Let cool slightly.

3 Meanwhile, cream the butter and half the sugar until light and fluffy. Beat in the melted chocolate, then the egg yolks, one at a time.

4 Beat the egg whites in a separate bowl until they form stiff peaks, then gradually beat in the remaining sugar.

5 Stir half the egg whites into the chocolate mixture to loosen it slightly.

6 Sift the flour and almonds together, then fold in with the remaining egg white.

7 Spoon the mixture into the prepared pan and bake until a skewer inserted in the center comes out clean, 50 to 60 minutes.

8 Let cool about 10 minutes. Then remove from the pan and cool completely on a wire rack.

9 To make the frosting, heat the cream in a saucepan until nearly boiling. Remove from the heat and stir in the chocolate until melted, then stir in the orange peel. Keep stirring until the frosting thickens.

10 Spoon the mixture over the cake and spread evenly over the top and sides. Let the frosting set before dusting with the confectioners' sugar.

According to legend, **devil's food cake** got its characteristic red color—and hence its name—because a chemical reaction between baking soda and early varieties of cocoa turned it red during cooking. It is more likely that red food coloring was used to turn the cake red and that the cake's name simply comes from the fact that **it is so wickedly rich and sinfully chocolaty!**

Angel Food Cake

A real party favorite and a truly magnificent feat of the art of cake-making, this cake is held together almost purely by air.

Serves 8–10

1/3 cup (55 g) all-purpose flour
1 tbsp. cornstarch
scant 1 cup (200 g) sugar
7 egg whites
3/4 tsp. cream of tartar
pinch of salt
1 1/2 tsp. vanilla extract

Frosting
2 egg whites
1 1/2 cups (350 g) sugar
1/4 tsp. cream of tartar
1/4 cup (60 ml) water
2 tbsp. chopped toasted pistachios, plus extra to decorate

1 Preheat the oven to 350°F (180°C, Gas 4). Grease and bottom-line a 9-in. (23-cm) springform tube pan.

2 Sift the flour and cornstarch together. Add half the sugar and sift together twice.

3 Beat the egg whites until foamy. Add the cream of tartar and salt and continue whisking until they form stiff peaks.

4 Beat the remaining sugar into the egg whites until stiff and glossy. Beat in the vanilla extract.

5 Fold in the flour mixture in three batches, then spoon the mixture into the prepared pan. The mixture should come up to the top. Smooth the top and bake until lightly golden and spongy to the touch, 45 to 50 minutes.

6 Remove from the oven and invert onto a wire rack. Let cool in the pan.

7 To make the frosting, put all the ingredients, except the pistachios, into a heatproof bowl. Set the bowl over a pan of simmering water. Beat with a hand-held electric mixer until thick, 10 to 12 minutes. Stir in the pistachios.

8 Run a knife around the sides of the pan and remove. Spread the frosting over the top. Finish with a sprinkling of pistachios.

The classic **angel food cake** is now so embedded in American culture that October 10 is set aside as National Angel Food Cake Day! The cake's origins are unclear, but it is thought to have originated in the 1870s in Pennsylvania—the area was one of the major producers of cake molds at this time. It has been suggested that the first angel food cake was baked at the Beer Hotel in St. Louis because it was available in the hotel's 1888 catalog. However, several recipes for the cake were available before this.

Angel food cake is a reworking of sponge and cornstarch cakes, but it contains absolutely no fat. This is probably how it got its unusual name: the angel food cake is deliciously light, airy, and innocent—a food fit for angels! The cake is a traditional taste of America and one of the county's most popular desserts, and, although its progress is slow, its appeal is beginning to spread around the world.

"There are few hours in life more agreeable than the hour dedicated to the ceremony known as afternoon tea."

Henry James

Black Cherry and Chocolate Cake

Enter this on the food roll of honor—the classic Black Forest Gateau graduates into this utterly enticing updated version that's perfect throughout the holiday season.

Serves 6–8

8 eggs
1 1/2 cups (175 g) all-purpose flour, sifted
1/2 cup (55 g) cocoa powder,
   plus extra for dusting

Filling
1 lb. 4 oz. (500 g) fresh black cherries,
   pitted
1/2 cup (125 ml) cherry liqueur or
   dark rum
3 1/2 cups (800 ml) heavy cream
14 oz. (400 g) semisweet chocolate,
   broken into pieces

1 Preheat the oven to 400°F (200°C, Gas 6). Line two 10 x 12-in. (25 x 30-cm) jelly roll pans with waxed paper.

2 Put the eggs in a large mixing bowl set over a saucepan of simmering water. Beat with an electric mixer until very thick and pale, 15 to 20 minutes.

3 Remove from the heat and fold in the flour and cocoa. Pour the mixture into the prepared pans and bake until golden and risen, 12 to 15 minutes. Let cool.

4 To make the filling, place the cherries in a bowl and pour the liqueur over. Heat the cream in a large saucepan. Place the chocolate in a large bowl and pour the hot cream over. Set aside 5 minutes, then stir until completely smooth. Chill about 45 minutes.

5 When the chocolate cream is cold, beat with an electric mixer for 5 to 10 minutes until thickened and pale.

6 Using a 10-in. (25-cm) springform pan as a template, cut rounds out of the chocolate cake. Line the bottom of the pan with one of the cake disks.

7 Arrange the cherries on top, spooning half the liqueur over as well. Cover with three-quarters of the chocolate cream and top with the second cake disk.

8 Spread the remaining chocolate cream over the top and dust with cocoa powder. Chill at least 45 minutes before serving.

The **Black Forest Gateau's** exact origins are unknown, but it is believed to have originated in Swabia in the Black Forest region of Germany in the 16th century. The area is well known for its sour cherries and kirsch (cherry brandy), and Germany has always been famous for its love of quality chocolate. Combining these ingredients into this delicious chocolate dessert seems almost to have been preordained!

Gooey Chocolate Cake

Sheer, outrageous indulgence—this cake is deliciously gooey and melts in the mouth; utterly irresistible whatever the occasion!

Serves 8–10

11 oz. (300 g) bittersweet chocolate, at least 50% cocoa solids, broken into pieces
3/4 cup (175 g) unsalted butter
8 eggs, separated
1 cup (200 g) packed light brown sugar
1/2 cup (60 g) ground almonds

Frosting
2/3 cup (150 g) unsalted butter
1 3/4 cups (225 g) confectioners' sugar
1/4 cup (30 g) cocoa powder, sifted
1–2 tbsp. hot water

1 Preheat the oven to 350°F (180°C, Gas 4). Grease an 8-in. (20-cm) springform pan, then wrap the base and sides of the pan with aluminum foil.

2 Melt the chocolate and butter in a large, heatproof bowl placed over a saucepan of simmering water. Let cool.

3 Beat the egg yolks with the sugar until thick and pale. Stir in the cooled chocolate and butter mixture, then the ground almonds.

4 Beat the egg whites until they form stiff peaks. Fold them into the chocolate mixture. Pour the mixture into the prepared pan, and place in a roasting pan half full of boiling water.

5 Bake until the cake is quite firm yet a skewer inserted in the center comes out a little sticky, 40 to 45 minutes. Let cool in the pan, then transfer the cake to a plate.

6 To make the frosting, melt the butter in a pan. Add the confectioners' sugar and cocoa powder and beat well. Add the water and beat until glossy. Let chill until the frosting has a spreadable consistency, about 15 minutes. Spread the frosting over the top and sides of the cake.

Glossary

The following culinary terms will provide useful guidelines
for international readers to follow.

U.S.	British	U.S.	British
all-purpose flour	plain flour	light cream	single cream
baking soda	bicarbonate of soda	molasses	black treacle
beat	whisk	packed brown sugar	muscovado sugar
bittersweet chocolate	bitter plain chocolate	pan	tin
bread flour	strong flour	paper baking cups	paper cases
cake pan	cake tin	peel	zest
confectioners' sugar	icing sugar	pie shell	pastry case
cornstarch	cornflour	plastic wrap	cling film
dessert apples	eating apples	semisweet chocolate	plain chocolate
extract	essence	shredded coconut	desiccated coconut
fast-acting yeast	easy-blend yeast	skillet	frying pan
golden raisins	sultanas	slivered almonds	flaked almonds
graham crackers	digestive biscuits	stone-ground cornmeal	fine polenta
heavy cream	double cream	sugar	caster sugar
jelly	jam	turbinado sugar	demerara sugar
jelly roll	Swiss roll	vanilla bean	vanilla pod
ladyfingers	sponge fingers	waxed paper	baking parchment
light corn syrup	golden syrup	whole wheat flour	wholemeal flour

Picture Credits

Index